UNLOCKING YOUR POTENTIALS

The Fundamental Principles Of Personal Growth

BOOK DESCRIPTION

Unlocking your potential growth is an empowering book that delves into the art of personal growth and achievement. it provides readers with the essential tools and strategies to unlock their inner capabilities and maximize their potential, through engaging stories, practical exercises, and thought-provoking insights. 'this book serves as a **COMPREHENSIVE ROADMAP** for individuals seeking to take charge of their lives, setting meaning and achievable goals, and overcoming self-limiting beliefs

BOOK CONENTS

Chapter 1: understanding personal growth.

i.   Importance of personal growth in one's life

ii.   Difference between fixed mindset and growth mindset

Chapter 2: Self-awareness and reflection

i.   The role of self-awareness in personal growth

ii. Practical tips for self-reflection and understanding one's strengths and weaknesses

iii. The importance of identifying limiting beliefs and how to overcome them

Chapter 3:setting meaning goals

i. Setting clear, meaningful, and achievable goals that align with values and aspirations

ii. The concepts of SMART goals

iii. Strategies for staying motivated and overcoming obstacles on the path to goal achievement

Chapter 4:cultivating positive habits

i. The power of habits in shaping one's life

ii. Key habits that promote personal growth, such as mindfulness, gratitude, and continuous learning

iii. Practical advice on how to maintain sustainable habits.

Chapter 5:building resilience and overcoming challenges

i. The inevitability of resilience and setbacks in life

ii. Strategies for building resilience and bouncing back stronger from difficult situations

iii. Inspiring stories of individuals who have overcome adversity through personal growth.

Chapter 6: Embracing change and adaptability

i. The importance of embracing change as a catalyst for personal growth

ii. Tips for developing adaptability and thriving in times of uncertainty

iii. The concept of growth mindset in facing new challenges

Chapter 7:nurturing positive relationships

i.   The influences of relationships in personal growth

ii. Tips to foster healthy, positive, and supportive relationships with family, friends, and colleagues

iii. The significance of setting boundaries and surrounding oneself with like-minded people.

Chapter 8: self-care and well-being

Key components to self-care and well-being

Conclusion.

CHAPTER ONE

<u>UNDERSTANDING PERSONAL GROWTH</u>

<u>POTENTIAL GROWTH</u>

This is the inherent capacity and capability within an individual to develop and improve in various aspects of life. It encompasses both personal and professional growth, encompassing areas such as skills, knowledge, talents, emotional intelligence, and character development. Potential growth is not fixed and can be nurtured and enhanced through learning, experiences, and self-improvement efforts.

Personal or potential growth is a lifelong journey. People who intentionally set out to enrich their lives through self-growth and development report that they are happier, more successful and have better relationships. It is important to understand that personal-growth is a self-motivated embarkation.

IMPORTANT OF POTENTIAL GROWTH IN ONE'S LIFE:

Be it intellectually, morally, physically or all of the above, potential growth is the direct results of efforts made to improve one's self. the importance of potential growth is achieved as follows:

Fulfillment and Satisfaction: Embracing and pursuing potential growth can lead to a greater sense of fulfillment and satisfaction in life. When individuals strive to reach their full potential, they experience a deeper sense of purpose and accomplishment.

Continuous Learning and Development: Potential growth drives individuals to seek new knowledge, acquire skills, and develop competencies. This commitment to continuous learning enables personal and professional growth, ensuring that individuals remain adaptable and relevant in an ever-changing world.

Career Advancement: In the professional realm, recognizing and harnessing one's potential can lead to career advancement and better job prospects. As individuals develop their skills and talents, they become more valuable assets in the workplace, opening doors to new opportunities and responsibilities.

Increased Confidence and Resilience: Embracing potential growth fosters self-confidence and resilience. As individuals overcome challenges and improve their abilities, they gain confidence in their capacity to handle future obstacles and navigate life's ups and downs with greater poise.

Enhanced Relationships: Potential growth positively impacts interpersonal relationships. As individuals develop emotional intelligence and self-awareness, they are better equipped to understand and empathize with others, leading to stronger connections and healthier interactions.

Personal Empowerment: Realizing one's potential empowers individuals to take charge of their lives and make positive changes. It instills a belief in their ability to shape their destiny and take control of their own happiness and success.

Positive Influence on Others: Embracing potential growth can serve as an inspiration to others. When individuals strive to reach their full potential, they become role models, encouraging and motivating those around them to pursue their own growth and development.

Adaptability and Resilience: In a rapidly changing world, potential growth enables individuals to adapt and thrive in new circumstances. The ability to learn, evolve, and embrace change makes individuals more resilient and better equipped to handle uncertainties.

Personal Transformation: The journey of potential growth is transformative. It leads individuals to discover their passions, strengths, and true potential, allowing them to lead more authentic and purpose-driven lives.

Long-Term Well-Being: Embracing potential growth is an investment in one's long-term well-being and happiness. As individuals continuously evolve and improve, they experience greater overall life satisfaction and a deeper sense of contentment.

BENEFITS OF PERSONAL DEVELOPMENT

Embarking on a journey of personal development can bring about a wide range of benefits that positively impact various aspects of your life. Here are some of the key benefits:

Self-awareness: Personal development encourages self-reflection, helping you gain a deeper understanding of your thoughts, emotions, and behaviors. This self-awareness enables you to recognize your strengths and weaknesses, allowing you to make informed decisions and focus on personal growth areas.

Increased confidence: As you develop new skills, overcome challenges, and achieve your goals, your confidence grows. This newfound self-assurance can positively influence all areas of your life, from work and relationships to pursuing new opportunities.

Improved goal setting: Personal development helps you clarify your aspirations and set meaningful, achievable goals. It provides you with the tools to break down larger objectives into smaller, manageable steps, making it easier to stay focused and motivated.

Enhanced resilience: Life is full of ups and downs, and personal development equips you with coping mechanisms and emotional resilience to navigate through difficult times. You become better equipped to handle stress, setbacks, and adversity with a more positive outlook.

Better relationships: As you work on your personal growth, you become more empathetic and understanding, leading to improved relationships with family, friends, and colleagues. You learn to communicate effectively, resolve conflicts, and cultivate deeper connections with others.

Increased productivity: Personal development often involves time management and organizational skills, leading to increased productivity and efficiency in both personal and professional endeavors.

Better health and well-being: Investing in personal development can have a positive impact on your physical and mental health. As you develop healthy habits and manage stress effectively, you may experience improved overall well-being.

Lifelong learning: Personal development is an ongoing process that encourages continuous learning and self-improvement. It opens your mind to new ideas, perspectives, and opportunities for growth throughout your life.

Greater fulfillment and purpose: By aligning your actions with your values and passions, personal development can lead to a sense of fulfillment and purpose in life. You may find deeper meaning in your pursuits and feel a stronger sense of contentment.

Improved decision-making: With increased self-awareness and clarity about your goals, personal development can lead to better decision-making. You become more adept at weighing options and considering the long-term consequences of your choices.

Enhanced creativity: Personal growth often involves exploring different aspects of yourself and the world around you, fostering creativity and innovative thinking.

Positive impact on others: As you grow and improve, you become an inspiration to those around you. Your positive changes may motivate others to embark on their own journeys of personal development.

Overall, the journey of personal development is a transformative and rewarding process that empowers you to lead a more fulfilling and purposeful life.

MINDSETS: FIXED VS GROWTH MINDSET

The terms "fixed mindset" and "growth mindset" were popularized by psychologist Carol Dweck through her research on achievement and success. They refer to two different beliefs or attitudes that people have towards their abilities and talents. These mindsets can significantly impact a person's approach to challenges, learning, and overall personal development.

Difference between fixed mindset and growth mindset

Here's a breakdown of the differences between a **fixed mindset** and a **growth mindset.**

<u>**Fixed Mindset:**</u>

In a fixed mindset, individuals believe that their abilities, intelligence, and talents are fixed traits. They think these qualities are innate and unchangeable.

People with a fixed mindset tend to avoid challenges because they fear failure, which they see as a reflection of their inherent limitations.

When faced with setbacks or obstacles, those with a fixed mindset often become discouraged and may give up easily, believing they lack the capacity to improve.

They might feel threatened or envious by the success of others because they interpret it as a validation of the other person's inherent superiority, rather than seeing it as a result of effort and learning.

Criticism or constructive feedback is often taken personally and defensively because they interpret it as a judgment of their inherent worth and intelligence.

Growth Mindset:

In a growth mindset, individuals believe that their abilities, intelligence, and talents can be developed and improved over time through effort, learning, and perseverance.

People with a growth mindset embrace challenges because they see them as opportunities for growth and learning. They are willing to take on new and difficult tasks, even if they might initially struggle.

When faced with setbacks, those with a growth mindset view them as a natural part of the learning process and use them as opportunities to learn, adapt, and improve.

They find inspiration in the success of others, seeing it as evidence that effort and hard work can lead to positive outcomes.

Criticism or feedback is seen as valuable information for growth, and they are more likely to use it constructively to improve their skills and abilities.

It's important to note that people can exhibit elements of both mindsets in different situations or areas of life. A person may have a growth mindset when it comes to academics but a fixed mindset in sports, for example. The good news is that mindsets are not fixed traits; they can be developed and changed with self-awareness, effort, and a willingness to challenge one's beliefs. Cultivating a growth mindset can lead to increased resilience, motivation, and a more positive attitude toward learning and personal development.

CHAPTER TWO

SELF AWARENESS AND REFLECTION

Self-Awareness in Personal Growth.

Self-awareness plays a paramount role in personal growth and development. It serves as the foundation upon which individuals can build meaningful and positive changes in their lives. Here's why self-awareness is crucial for personal growth:

Identification of Strengths and Weaknesses: Self-awareness enables individuals to recognize their strengths and capitalize on them, while also acknowledging their weaknesses and areas that need improvement. This understanding allows for a more focused approach to personal development, as one can work on enhancing their strengths and addressing their weaknesses.

Effective Goal Setting: When someone is self-aware, they can set more realistic and relevant goals aligned with their values, interests, and capabilities. This clarity increases the likelihood of achieving those objectives, leading to a sense of accomplishment and motivation to continue growing.

Improved Decision Making: Self-aware individuals are better equipped to make informed decisions. By understanding their emotions, biases, and thought processes, they can make more rational and considered choices, which often lead to better outcomes.

Enhanced Emotional Intelligence: Being self-aware allows people to identify and understand their emotions and reactions, as well as how they impact their behavior and relationships. This heightened emotional intelligence fosters healthier interactions with others and promotes empathy and understanding.

Adaptability and Resilience: Through self-awareness, individuals become more adaptable and resilient in the face of challenges and setbacks. They can acknowledge their emotional responses to adversity and employ coping strategies to navigate difficult situations effectively.

Continual Learning and Growth: Self-awareness facilitates a growth mindset, encouraging individuals to view challenges as opportunities for learning rather than failures. This mindset promotes continuous personal development and a willingness to embrace change and new experiences.

Authenticity and Self-Expression: Self-awareness enables people to better understand their values and beliefs, fostering authenticity in how they present themselves to the world. This authenticity leads to more genuine connections with others and a stronger sense of identity.

Effective Communication: Understanding one's communication style and patterns allows for improved interpersonal relationships. Self-aware individuals can express their thoughts and emotions more clearly, listen actively, and communicate with empathy, resulting in healthier and more meaningful connections.

Reduced Self-Doubt and Anxiety: Self-awareness helps individuals recognize and challenge negative thought patterns and self-doubt. By understanding the source of their insecurities, they can work towards building self-confidence and reducing anxiety.

Empowerment and Accountability: Taking ownership of one's actions and behaviors is a vital aspect of personal growth. Self-awareness empowers individuals to accept responsibility for their choices and take proactive steps towards positive change.

In summary, self-awareness acts as a compass that guides personal growth and development. It fosters a deeper understanding of oneself and others, paving the way for a more fulfilling and purpose-driven life. By cultivating self-awareness, individuals can embark on a transformative journey of continuous improvement and self-discovery.

THE ROLE OF SELF-AWARENESS IN PERSONAL GROWTH.

The role of self awareness in personal growth is discussed as follows:

Increased Accountability: When individuals are self-aware, they take responsibility for their actions and decisions. They acknowledge their role in both successes and failures, which promotes a proactive attitude towards personal growth and learning from experiences.

Adaptability and Flexibility: Self-awareness allows individuals to adapt and respond better to changing circumstances. By understanding their own reactions and behavioral patterns, they can make conscious efforts to modify their responses and adapt to new situations more effectively.

Stress Management: Self-awareness helps in recognizing stress triggers and understanding how stress affects physical and emotional well-being. With this awareness, individuals can adopt coping strategies and relaxation techniques to manage stress more effectively.

Empowerment and Authenticity: Self-awareness fosters self-acceptance and authenticity. When individuals understand and accept themselves, they can live and express their values and beliefs genuinely, leading to a greater sense of empowerment and fulfillment.

PRACTICAL TIPS FOR SELF REFLECTION AND UNDERSTANDING ONE'S STRENGTHS AND WEAKNESSES

Practicing self-reflection and understanding one's strengths and weaknesses are essential steps towards self-awareness and personal growth. Here are some practical tips to help you develop these skills:

Journaling: Set aside time each day or week to write in a journal. Reflect on your experiences, emotions, and reactions to different situations. Writing allows you to process your thoughts and gain insights into your behaviors and patterns.

Ask for Feedback: Seek feedback from trusted friends, family members, or colleagues. They can offer valuable perspectives on your strengths and weaknesses that you might not see from your own vantage point.

Take Personality and Strengths Assessments: Consider taking personality assessments like the Myers-Briggs Type Indicator (MBTI) or strengths assessments like the Clifton-strengths to gain deeper insights into your personality traits and unique talents.

Mindfulness and Meditation: Practice mindfulness and meditation to become more present and aware of your thoughts and emotions. This can help you identify recurring patterns and triggers that influence your actions.

Self-Questioning: Regularly ask yourself introspective questions such as:

What are my core values and beliefs?

What activities make me feel energized and fulfilled?

In which areas do I excel, and why?

What are the areas where I struggle, and what might be the reasons behind it?

Seek Diverse Experiences: Engage in new and diverse experiences to discover your interests, strengths, and weaknesses. Trying different activities can lead to a better understanding of your capabilities.

Embrace Feedback Positively: When receiving feedback, approach it with an open mind and a willingness to learn. Avoid becoming defensive and instead, focus on understanding the insights it offers.

Set Specific Goals: Define clear and achievable goals that align with your strengths and interests. Regularly assess your progress and make adjustments based on what you learn about yourself along the way.

Reflect on Challenges and Mistakes: Instead of dwelling on mistakes, view them as opportunities for growth. Analyze what led to those challenges and how you can handle similar situations better in the future.

Practice Self-Compassion: Be kind and understanding towards yourself throughout this process. Recognize that self-awareness is a journey, and it's okay to have strengths and weaknesses—everyone does.

Use Technology: Use apps or online tools: There are various apps and online tools available that can help you track your habits, emotions, and progress, which can provide valuable data for self-reflection.

Join a Supportive Community: Engage with like-minded individuals who value personal growth. Join workshops, discussion groups, or online forums where you can share experiences and learn from others.

Remember, self-awareness is an ongoing practice, and it requires dedication and patience. Regularly engaging in self-reflection and understanding your strengths and weaknesses can lead to a deeper understanding of yourself, improved decision-making, and ultimately, personal growth and fulfillment.

OVERCOMING LIMITING BELIEFS.

The Importance Of Identifying Limiting Beliefs And How To Overcome Them

Limiting beliefs are negative thought patterns or assumptions that hold individuals back from pursuing their goals and realizing their true capabilities. These beliefs often stem from past experiences, societal conditioning, or negative feedback, and they can severely hinder progress and success in various aspects of life. Identifying and overcoming limiting beliefs is crucial for personal growth, self-improvement, and achieving one's full potential. Here's why it's important to identify and overcome limiting beliefs:

Self-fulfilling prophecy: Limiting beliefs can become self-fulfilling prophecies, meaning that if you believe you can't achieve something, you are less likely to take the necessary actions to succeed. As a result, you're more likely to confirm your belief and remain stuck in a cycle of unfulfilled potential.

Lack of confidence: Limiting beliefs erode self-confidence and self-esteem. They make you doubt your abilities, which can lead to missed opportunities and reluctance to step out of your comfort zone.

Missed opportunities: When you believe you're not capable of something, you may avoid trying altogether, missing out on valuable opportunities for growth and success.

Impact on relationships: Limiting beliefs can affect how you perceive others and how you interact with them. These beliefs may lead to a negative outlook, making it challenging to build meaningful and positive relationships.

Stagnation: Limiting beliefs can create a sense of complacency, preventing you from striving for more in life and settling for less than you deserve.

STRATEGIES TO OVERCOMING LIMITING BELIEFS:

Self-awareness: The first step is to identify and acknowledge your limiting beliefs. Pay attention to negative thought patterns and self-talk that may be holding you back. Keep a journal to record these beliefs and their impact on your life.

Question your beliefs: Challenge the validity of your limiting beliefs by asking yourself for evidence supporting or refuting them. Often, you'll find that these beliefs lack a solid foundation and are based on assumptions rather than facts.

Positive affirmations: Replace limiting beliefs with positive affirmations. Affirmations are statements that reinforce positive thoughts and behaviors. Repeat them daily to rewire your thought patterns.

Visualize your success: Imagine yourself successfully overcoming challenges and achieving your goals. Visualization can help reprogram your mind and increase your confidence.

Seek professional support if needed: Share your limiting beliefs with a trusted friend, family member, or a professional counselor. Sometimes an outside perspective can help you gain new insights and challenge your beliefs.

Take action: Break down your goals into smaller, achievable steps. As you take action and see progress, you'll build confidence and weaken the grip of limiting beliefs.

Embrace failure as learning: Fear of failure often fuels limiting beliefs. Instead, view failures as opportunities for growth and learning. Analyze what went wrong, make adjustments, and try again.

Surround yourself with positivity: Surround yourself with supportive and positive influences, such as inspirational books, podcasts, or motivational speakers. Positive environments can reinforce a growth mindset.

Remember, overcoming limiting beliefs is a process that takes time and effort. Be patient and compassionate with yourself as you work towards transforming your mindset and unleashing your true potential.

CHAPTER THREE

SETTING MEANINGFUL GOALS

Setting Clear And Achievable Goals That Aligns With Values And Aspirations.

Setting clear and achievable goals that align with your values and aspirations is crucial for personal growth and success. Here are some guides to help you in this process:

Self-Reflection and Identify Values:

Take some time for self-reflection and identify your core values. What is truly important to you in life? What do you want to prioritize? Understanding your values will give your goals a meaningful foundation.

Visualize Your Aspirations:

Envision your ideal future and the person you want to become. Visualizing your aspirations can give you a clearer picture of the goals you need to set to reach that destination.

Set Specific Goals:

Make your goals as specific as possible. Avoid vague statements and define exactly what you want to achieve. Specific goals are easier to measure and track progress.

Use the SMART Criteria:

Employ the SMART criteria to set goals:

Specific: Clearly define what you want to accomplish.

Measurable: Establish how you will track your progress.

Achievable: Ensure that your goals are realistic and attainable.

Relevant: Align your goals with your values and aspirations.

Time-bound: Set a deadline to create a sense of urgency.

Break Goals into Smaller Steps:

Divide your bigger goals into smaller, manageable steps. This makes them less overwhelming and allows you to track your progress more effectively.

Prioritize Goals:

Focus on a few essential goals at a time. Setting too many goals at once can lead to spreading yourself too thin and decreasing your chances of success.

Write Down Your Goals:

Putting your goals in writing reinforces your commitment to them. Use a journal, a planner, or digital tools to keep track of your goals and progress.

Stay Flexible:

Life is unpredictable, and circumstances may change. Be open to adjusting your goals as needed while staying true to your values and aspirations.

Develop an Action Plan:

Create a detailed action plan that outlines the steps you need to take to achieve each goal. Include deadlines, resources required, and potential obstacles with corresponding solutions.

Seek Accountability and Support:

Share your goals with a trusted friend, family member, or mentor who can provide encouragement, feedback, and keep you accountable.

Celebrate Milestones:

Celebrate your achievements along the way. Recognizing your progress, no matter how small, will keep you motivated and reinforce your commitment to your values and aspirations.

Stay Positive and Persistent:

Maintaining a positive attitude and being persistent in the face of challenges will help you overcome obstacles and stay on track toward your goals.

Remember, the journey of goal-setting and achievement is as important as the destination. Stay true to your values, be kind to yourself, and enjoy the process of growth and self-improvement.

MOTIVATION & OVERCOMING OBSTACLES.

Strategies For Staying Motivated And Overcoming Obstacles On The Path To Goal Achievement.

Staying motivated and overcoming obstacles on the path to goal achievement can be challenging, but with the right strategies, you can maintain focus and persevere. here are some effective techniques to help you stay motivated and tackle obstacles:

Set Clear And Specific Goals: Start by defining your goals in a clear and specific manner. Having well-defined objectives gives you a clear direction to follow, making it easier to stay focused and motivated.

Break Goals Into Smaller Steps: Divide your larger goals into smaller, manageable tasks. This approach allows you to track your progress more effectively and gives you a sense of accomplishment as you complete each step.

Create a plan: Develop a detailed plan with deadlines and milestones. Having a roadmap will help you stay organized and provide structure to your journey towards achieving your goals.

Visualize success: Imagine yourself successfully accomplishing your goals. Visualization can be a powerful tool to boost motivation and reinforce your determination to overcome obstacles.

Maintain a positive mindset: Cultivate a positive attitude and believe in your abilities. Positive thinking can help you stay resilient in the face of challenges.

Celebrate progress: Acknowledge and celebrate your achievements, no matter how small they may seem. Celebrating milestones provides positive reinforcement and encourages you to keep going.

Seek inspiration: Surround yourself with motivational content, books, podcasts, or inspiring individuals who have achieved similar goals. Learning from their experiences can keep you motivated and provide valuable insights.

Stay flexible: Be open to adjusting your approach if you encounter obstacles. Flexibility allows you to adapt to changing circumstances and find alternative solutions.

Share your goals with friends, family, or a mentor who can hold you accountable. Having someone to support and encourage you can make a significant difference in staying motivated.

Learn from setbacks: Instead of seeing obstacles as failures, view them as opportunities to learn and grow. Analyze what went wrong, and use that knowledge to improve your future efforts.

Practice self-compassion: Be kind to yourself during the journey. It's normal to face challenges and have setbacks. Treat yourself with the same understanding and encouragement you would offer to a friend.

Stay organized and manage time: Organize your workspace and manage your time efficiently. Being organized can reduce distractions and help you stay focused on your goals.

Avoid overwhelm: Sometimes, the path to achieving a goal can feel overwhelming. Break tasks into smaller, manageable portions to prevent feeling discouraged.

Take breaks and practice self-care: Burnout can hinder motivation, so make sure to take breaks and practice self-care. Engage in activities that help you relax and recharge.

Keep a journal: Document your progress, thoughts, and emotions in a journal. This can help you gain insights into your journey and identify patterns that may be affecting your motivation.

Remember that staying motivated is an ongoing process, and it's normal to face challenges along the way. Be patient with yourself and use these strategies consistently to build resilience and overcome obstacles on your path to goal.

CHAPTER FOUR

<u>CULTIVATING POSITIVE HABITS</u>

Cultivating positive habits is an essential aspect of personal growth and development. By establishing positive habits, we can improve our well-being, productivity, and overall quality of life. Here are some steps to help you cultivate positive habits:

Identify your goals: Determine what specific positive habits you want to develop. Whether it's exercising regularly, eating healthier, practicing mindfulness, reading more, or being more organized, clarity about your goals is crucial.

Start small: Don't try to overhaul your entire life overnight. Begin with small, achievable changes. By starting small, you reduce the chances of feeling overwhelmed and increase your chances of success.

Be consistent: Consistency is key to forming habits. Commit to your new habits on a daily or regular basis. Consistency helps solidify the habit and makes it more likely to become a natural part of your routine.

Create a routine: Incorporate your positive habits into an existing routine or build a new one around them. Having a structured schedule makes it easier to stick to your habits and ensures you allocate time for them.

Set reminders: In the beginning, it can be helpful to set reminders to prompt you to practice your positive habits. Use alarms, sticky notes, or digital apps to keep you on track until the habits become more ingrained.

Track your progress: Keep a journal or use habit-tracking apps to monitor your progress. Seeing your improvement and how far you've come can be motivating and reinforce your commitment to the positive habits.

Stay accountable: Share your goals with a friend, family member, or join a community of people with similar aspirations. Accountability partners can provide support, encouragement, and help you stay on track.

Stay positive and patient: Forming new habits takes time, and setbacks are a normal part of the process. Be kind to yourself and avoid self-criticism if you miss a day or encounter difficulties. Focus on the progress you make rather than perfection.

Reward yourself: Celebrate your successes, no matter how small they may seem. Rewarding yourself positively reinforces the habit and makes you associate positive feelings with the behavior.

Learn from mistakes: If you find yourself falling back into old patterns, use it as an opportunity to learn. Identify what triggered the lapse and develop strategies to overcome those challenges in the future.

Incorporate enjoyment: Try to find joy in the process of developing positive habits. If you enjoy what you're doing, you're more likely to stick with it in the long run.

Review and adjust: Regularly review your habits and their impact on your life. Be open to adjusting or refining them as needed. As your life circumstances change, your habits may need to evolve too.

Remember that *forming positive habits is an ongoing journey,* and it's okay to take it *one step at a time.* Embrace the process and be patient with yourself as you work towards positive change in your life.

THE POWER OF HABITS IN SHAPING ONE'S LIFE

Habits are repetitive behaviors or actions that we perform almost automatically, often without much conscious thought. They are formed through a loop of cue, routine, and reward, which reinforces their recurrence, and as such, **can not be overstated.** The impact of habits on an individual's life is profound, and here are some key aspects to understand their significance:

Consistency and compound effect: Habits are about consistency and repetition. Small actions performed consistently over time can lead to significant changes in one's life. The compound effect of positive habits can lead to substantial improvements in various aspects, such as health, relationships, career, and personal growth.

Automated behavior: Habits free up mental energy and willpower because they become ingrained and automatic. When something becomes a habit, it no longer requires a great deal of conscious effort to perform, which allows individuals to focus on other tasks and challenges.

Personal development: Positive habits contribute to personal development and self-improvement. Engaging in habits that promote learning, self-reflection, and skill-building can lead to continuous growth and development.

Goal achievement: Habits play a crucial role in achieving long-term goals. By incorporating habits that align with specific objectives, individuals create a path of progress toward their desired outcomes.

Emotional regulation: Certain habits can help manage stress, anxiety, and other emotions. For instance, practicing mindfulness or regular exercise can have positive effects on mental well-being and emotional regulation.

Health and well-being: Health-related habits, such as a balanced diet, regular exercise, and sufficient sleep, significantly impact physical and mental health. Healthy habits contribute to increased energy levels, improved immune function, and a reduced risk of various diseases.

Time management: Habits can improve time management by creating structured routines and optimizing productivity. Efficient daily habits can lead to better time utilization and prevent procrastination.

Social and relationship impact: Habits influence how individuals interact with others. Positive habits, such as active listening, empathy, and communication skills, can foster healthier and more meaningful relationships.

Breaking bad habits: On the other hand, recognizing and breaking negative habits is equally crucial. Destructive habits can hinder personal growth and lead to adverse consequences in various life areas.

Self-identity: Habits are closely linked to an individual's self-identity. The habits a person develops and maintains can shape their perception of themselves, reinforcing either positive or negative self-concepts.

Recognizing the power of habits allows individuals to be more intentional in shaping their lives. By identifying beneficial habits to adopt and harmful ones to eliminate, people can take control of their behaviors and work towards becoming the best version of themselves. It's essential to understand that habits are not formed overnight and require patience and persistence, but the long-term impact on one's life makes the effort well worthwhile.

Key habits that promote personal growth, such as mindfulness, gratitude, and continuous learning.

Absolutely! Personal growth is a lifelong journey, and cultivating certain habits can greatly contribute to your development and overall well-being.

Here are some key habits that promote personal growth:

Mindfulness: Practicing mindfulness involves being fully present in the moment, observing your thoughts and feelings without judgment. It can help reduce stress, improve focus, and enhance self-awareness.

Gratitude: Regularly expressing gratitude for the positive aspects of your life can shift your focus towards the good and help you develop a more positive outlook. Keeping a gratitude journal or simply taking a moment each day to reflect on what you're grateful for can be very beneficial.

Continuous learning: Embrace a growth mindset and stay open to learning new things. This could involve taking up new hobbies, reading books, attending workshops, or pursuing formal education. Learning keeps your mind engaged and adaptable.

Goal setting: Set clear and achievable goals for yourself. Having specific targets to work towards gives you direction and a sense of purpose. Break down larger goals into smaller, manageable steps to track progress and stay motivated.

Self-reflection: Regularly take time to reflect on your actions, decisions, and experiences. Honest self-assessment allows you to identify areas for improvement and make necessary changes.

Physical well-being: Taking care of your body through regular exercise, proper nutrition, and sufficient rest is crucial for personal growth. Physical well-being impacts your mental and emotional health as well.

Meditation and mindful breathing: Practicing meditation and mindful breathing can help reduce stress, improve focus, and enhance emotional regulation.

Embracing challenges: Be open to stepping out of your comfort zone and embracing challenges. Facing and overcoming obstacles can lead to significant personal growth.

Seeking feedback: Ask for feedback from trusted friends, family, or mentors. Constructive criticism can provide valuable insights and help you identify blind spots.

Self-compassion: Treat yourself with kindness and understanding. Acknowledge that everyone makes mistakes, and use setbacks as opportunities for learning and growth.

Time management: Develop effective time management skills to prioritize tasks and make the most of your time. This helps you avoid feeling overwhelmed and maintain a balanced life.

Empathy and compassion: Cultivate empathy and compassion towards others. Understanding and connecting with different perspectives can lead to personal growth and improved relationships.

Letting go of negativity: Practice letting go of grudges, negative thoughts, and limiting beliefs. Holding onto negativity can hinder personal growth and happiness.

Building resilience: Life is full of challenges and setbacks, but building resilience allows you to bounce back stronger from difficult situations.

Surrounding yourself with positive influences: Spend time with people who inspire and support you. Positive influences can motivate and encourage personal growth.

Remember that personal growth is not about perfection, but rather progress. Be patient with yourself and embrace the journey of continuous self-improvement.

POSITIVE HABIT BUILDING.

Practical advice on how to build sustainable positive habits.

Building and sustaining positive habits can significantly improve your life and well-being. Here are some practical pieces of advice to help you on your journey:

Start small: Begin with tiny habits that are easy to integrate into your daily routine. Gradually increase the complexity and difficulty as you build momentum.

Set clear goals: Define specific and realistic goals for the habits you want to develop. Having a clear target will give you direction and motivation.

Be consistent: Consistency is key to forming habits. Try to perform the habit at the same time and place every day, as this helps create a strong association in your mind.

Create reminders: Set up reminders, alarms, or calendar events to prompt you to perform your habit. Technology can be helpful for this purpose.

Accountability partner: Share your habit-building journey with a friend or family member who can hold you accountable and provide encouragement.

Track your progress: Use a habit tracker or journal to record your daily efforts. Seeing your progress can be motivating and help you stay on track.

Celebrate success: Acknowledge and reward yourself when you successfully stick to your habit. Positive reinforcement reinforces the habit loop.

Identify triggers and barriers: Be aware of triggers that can lead you to perform negative habits and identify potential barriers that may hinder your positive habit development. Find ways to avoid or overcome them.

Practice mindfulness: Mindfulness can help you become more aware of your actions and reactions. It enables you to make conscious choices and stay focused on your positive habits.

Learn from setbacks: It's normal to face setbacks along the way. Instead of being discouraged, view them as opportunities to learn and grow. Analyze what went wrong and make adjustments accordingly.

Visualize your success: Imagine yourself successfully carrying out your positive habit regularly. Visualization can strengthen your commitment and belief in your ability to achieve it.

Find purpose and meaning: Connect your positive habits to a broader purpose or goal that aligns with your values. Understanding why you're building a habit can give it more significance.

Avoid being overwhelm: Limit the number of new habits you try to build simultaneously. Focusing on one or a few at a time increases your chances of success.

Make it enjoyable: Find ways to make the habit enjoyable or rewarding. When you associate pleasure with the habit, you'll be more likely to stick with it.

Be patient: Building habits takes time and effort. Be patient with yourself, and don't get discouraged if progress is slow. Stay committed, and you'll see results over time.

Remember, the key to success lies in consistent effort and a positive mindset. Celebrate every small victory and keep pushing forward, even if you encounter obstacles along the way. Building positive habits can lead to a more fulfilling and successful life.

CHAPTER FIVE

<u>BUILDING RESILIENCE AND OVERCOMING CHALLENGES.</u>

Building resilience and overcoming challenges are essential skills that can help individuals navigate through life's ups and downs with strength and adaptability. Resilience is the ability to bounce back from setbacks, cope with adversity, and grow stronger in the face of challenges. Here are some tips and strategies to build resilience and overcome challenges:

Cultivate a positive mindset: A positive outlook can help you approach challenges with optimism and see opportunities in difficult situations. Focus on what you can control and try to reframe negative thoughts into more positive and constructive ones.

Develop a strong support system: Surround yourself with supportive and understanding friends, family members, or mentors. Having a network of people who can offer encouragement, guidance, and empathy can make a significant difference when facing challenges.

Practice self-care: Take care of your physical and emotional well-being. Regular exercise, a balanced diet, sufficient sleep, and relaxation techniques like meditation can help reduce stress and improve your resilience.

Set realistic goals: Break down larger goals into smaller, achievable steps. Celebrate each milestone you reach, as it will boost your confidence and motivation to overcome more significant challenges.

Learn from setbacks: Instead of dwelling on failures, see them as opportunities for learning and growth. Analyze what went wrong, what you can do differently next time, and use these insights to improve your approach.

Maintain flexibility and adaptability: Life is unpredictable, and being able to adapt to change is crucial for resilience. Develop the ability to adjust your plans and expectations as circumstances evolve.

Seek solutions and take action: When faced with challenges, don't get stuck in a state of helplessness. Take proactive steps towards finding solutions and taking action, no matter how small the steps may be.

Practice mindfulness: Mindfulness involves being present in the moment without judgment. It can help reduce stress and improve your ability to handle challenges with a clearer and calmer mindset.

Seek professional help if needed: Sometimes, challenges can be overwhelming, and seeking support from a therapist, counselor, or coach can provide valuable guidance and coping strategies.

Maintain a sense of humor: Humor can be a powerful tool in difficult times. Finding moments to laugh, even in the face of adversity, can lighten the emotional burden and help you keep a positive perspective.

Learn from others: Read or listen to stories of people who have overcome challenges or faced adversity. Their experiences and coping strategies can provide inspiration and valuable insights.

Celebrate your strengths: Recognize and celebrate your own strengths and achievements. Remind yourself of the challenges you've already overcome and the resilience you've demonstrated in the past.

Remember, building resilience is an ongoing process, and it takes time and practice. Embrace the journey, and with each challenge you overcome, you'll become stronger and more equipped to face whatever life throws your way.

THE INEVITABILITY OF CHALLENGES AND SETBACKS IN LIFE.

The inevitability of challenges and setbacks in life is a fundamental aspect of the human experience. No matter who we are or where we come from, life presents us with a series of obstacles and difficulties that we must navigate. These challenges can manifest in various forms, such as personal, professional, health-related, or interpersonal issues. Understanding and accepting the inevitability of these obstacles can help us better cope with them and lead more fulfilling lives.

Several factors contributing to the inevitability of challenges and setbacks:

Complexity of life: Life is inherently complex and unpredictable. It involves interactions with numerous variables, people, and circumstances. As a result, unexpected challenges can arise at any time.

Personal growth and learning: Challenges and setbacks are opportunities for personal growth and learning. They teach us valuable lessons, help us develop resilience, and provide insights into our strengths and weaknesses.

Changing circumstances: Life is in a constant state of change, and with change comes the possibility of both positive and negative outcomes. Even in the best of times, there will always be unforeseen circumstances that can lead to setbacks.

Human nature: As humans, we are not perfect, and we make mistakes. These mistakes can lead to setbacks in various aspects of our lives.

External factors: Many challenges are beyond our control, such as natural disasters, economic downturns, or the actions of other people. These external factors can have a significant impact on our lives.

Pursuit of goals: Setting and striving for goals is an essential part of life. However, the path to achieving these goals is seldom straightforward, and setbacks may occur along the way.

While challenges and setbacks are inevitable, it is essential to recognize that they do not define our entire existence. How we respond to these challenges plays a crucial role in shaping our lives. Some strategies for dealing with setbacks include:

Resilience: Developing resilience allows us to bounce back from setbacks, adapt to change, and maintain a positive outlook.

Problem-solving: Focusing on finding solutions to challenges rather than dwelling on the problems can help us overcome obstacles more effectively.

Seeking support: It's essential to lean on friends, family, or professional support when facing significant challenges. Sharing our burdens can make them feel more manageable.

Learning from setbacks: Viewing setbacks as learning opportunities can help us grow and make better choices in the future.

Self-compassion: Being kind to ourselves during challenging times and recognizing that setbacks are a natural part of life can reduce self-blame and negative self-judgment.

In conclusion, challenges and setbacks are an inherent part of the human journey. Embracing this reality and adopting a proactive and resilient approach to life can empower us to navigate through difficult times and ultimately lead to personal growth and fulfillment.

Strategies for building resilience and bouncing back stronger from difficult situations.

Building resilience is a valuable skill that enables individuals to cope with and bounce back from difficult situations. Here are some strategies to help you cultivate resilience and come back stronger:

Cultivate a positive mindset: Train your mind to focus on the positive aspects of situations, even in challenging times. Adopting an optimistic outlook can help you reframe difficulties as opportunities for growth and learning.

Practice mindfulness and self-awareness: Mindfulness allows you to stay present and observe your emotions without judgment. Being self-aware helps you recognize your emotional responses and thought patterns, enabling you to respond more effectively to stressors.

Develop a strong support network: Surround yourself with supportive and understanding individuals who can offer encouragement, empathy, and practical assistance when needed.

Set realistic goals: Break down larger challenges into smaller, achievable goals. Celebrate your progress along the way, as accomplishing smaller goals can boost your confidence and motivation.

Maintain physical well-being: Regular exercise, a balanced diet, and sufficient sleep contribute to overall well-being and can enhance your ability to cope with stress.

Learn from adversity: Embrace challenges as opportunities for growth. After a difficult situation, take time to reflect on what you've learned and how it has made you stronger or more knowledgeable.

Develop problem-solving skills: Enhance your ability to tackle problems effectively. Break down complex issues into manageable parts and explore different solutions.

Practice emotional regulation: Learn healthy ways to manage and express your emotions. Techniques like deep breathing, meditation, or journaling can help you process feelings in a constructive manner.

Maintain a sense of humor: Laughter can be a powerful tool for stress relief and perspective. Find moments of levity even in tough times.

Practice flexibility and adaptability: Life is full of uncertainties, and being able to adapt to changes is crucial. Cultivate a flexible mindset that allows you to adjust your plans and expectations as needed.

Seek professional help if necessary: There's no shame in seeking support from a therapist or counselor during challenging times. They can provide valuable guidance and coping strategies.

Engage in hobbies and activities you enjoy: Taking time for activities you love can serve as a form of self-care and stress relief, helping you recharge and maintain a positive outlook.

Volunteer or help others: Engaging in acts of kindness and helping others can provide a sense of purpose and fulfillment, boosting your own well-being in the process.

Develop resilience through past experiences: Reflect on past difficult situations you've overcome. Remind yourself of your resilience and strength in navigating those challenges.

Remember that building resilience is a process that takes time and practice. Be patient with yourself and celebrate your progress, no matter how small it may seem. By actively cultivating resilience, you'll be better equipped to face future difficulties with confidence and bounce back stronger.

Inspiring stories of individuals who have overcome adversity through personal growth.

There are countless inspiring stories of individuals who have overcome adversity through personal growth. Here are a few of them:

Helen keller: Helen keller was deaf and blind from an early age due to an illness. Despite her challenges, she learned to communicate through touch and went on to become the first deaf-blind person to earn a bachelor's degree. She became an author, lecturer, and advocate for people with disabilities, inspiring millions with her determination and resilience.

Nick vujicic: Born without limbs, nick vujicic faced severe physical challenges and emotional struggles growing up. However, he refused to let his disabilities define him. He became a motivational speaker, author, and founded an organization to support people facing similar obstacles. Nick's positive attitude and unwavering spirit have inspired many worldwide.

Malala yousafzai: Malala is a pakistani education activist who stood up for girls' rights to education in her home region of swat valley, where the taliban had banned girls from attending school. In 2012, she survived an assassination attempt and continued her advocacy despite the threat to her life. Malala became the youngest-ever nobel prize laureate, using her voice to advocate for education and gender equality.

J.k. Rowling: Before becoming the world-renowned author of the "Harry potter" Series, j.k. Rowling faced numerous rejections from publishers while struggling as a single mother living on welfare. She didn't give up on her dream and persisted through adversity. Her perseverance and creativity eventually led her to write one of the most beloved book series of all time.

Nelson mandela: Nelson mandela was an anti-apartheid revolutionary and political leader in south africa. He spent 27 years in prison for his efforts to end racial segregation and inequality. Instead of harboring bitterness, mandela focused on reconciliation and forgiveness after his release. He went on to become the first black president of south africa and worked to unite the nation, earning him worldwide admiration.

Oprah winfrey: Oprah faced a difficult upbringing, marked by poverty and abuse. Despite her challenging circumstances, she persevered and found success as a media mogul, talk show host, actress, and philanthropist. Oprah used her platform to inspire others and advocate for various social causes.

Stephen hawking: Renowned physicist stephen hawking was diagnosed with a rare motor neuron disease at the age of 21, which gradually paralyzed him. Despite his physical limitations, he continued his groundbreaking work in theoretical physics and cosmology, becoming one of the most brilliant minds of his time.

These individuals demonstrate the power of personal growth, resilience, and determination in overcoming adversity and achieving greatness. Their stories serve as a reminder that challenges can be opportunities for growth and positive change.

CHAPTER SIX

EMBRACING CHANGE AND ADAPTABILITY

Embracing change and adaptability is crucial in both personal and professional aspects of life. In today's rapidly changing world, being open and flexible to change can lead to personal growth, success, and overall well-being. Here are some reasons why embracing change and adaptability is important:

Coping with uncertainty: Change is an inherent part of life, and it often brings uncertainty. Embracing change allows us to become more resilient and better equipped to handle unforeseen challenges and situations.

Continuous growth and learning: Embracing change means being open to new experiences and ideas. This mindset fosters continuous learning and personal development, leading to a more enriching life.

Enhanced problem-solving skills: When you are adaptable, you can quickly adjust your thinking and approach when faced with problems. This flexibility enables you to find innovative solutions and overcome obstacles effectively.

Remaining relevant in the workplace: In a rapidly evolving job market, adaptability is a sought-after skill by employers. Those who can adapt to new technologies, trends, and ways of working are more likely to stay relevant and valuable to their organizations.

Building stronger relationships: Embracing change often involves interacting with new people or experiencing different social situations. It can help you build empathy, understanding, and better communication skills, leading to stronger and more diverse relationships.

Reducing stress: Resisting change can lead to increased stress and anxiety. Embracing change, on the other hand, allows you to go with the flow, which can significantly reduce stress levels and improve overall well-being.

Seizing opportunities: Change can bring unexpected opportunities, and those who are adaptable and open to new possibilities are more likely to recognize and seize these chances for personal and professional growth.

Tips for embracing change and adaptability:

Cultivate a growth mindset: See challenges and setbacks as opportunities to learn and improve. Embrace the idea that your abilities and intelligence can be developed with dedication and hard work.

Stay curious: Be open to exploring new things and seeking out new knowledge. Curiosity keeps the mind engaged and helps you adapt to new situations more effectively.

Develop flexibility: Practice being flexible in your thinking and approach. Be willing to consider different perspectives and be open to change when necessary.

Take calculated risks: While change can be uncertain, taking calculated risks can lead to valuable experiences and personal growth.

Build a support system: Surround yourself with supportive and positive people who can encourage and guide you through times of change.

Practice mindfulness: Being mindful helps you stay present and focused, enabling you to adapt more effectively to new situations as they arise.

Celebrate small wins: Acknowledge and celebrate your progress in adapting to change, no matter how small. Positive reinforcement can help you stay motivated.

Remember that change is constant, and the ability to adapt is a skill that can be cultivated and strengthened over time. Embracing change with a positive and open attitude can lead to a more fulfilling and successful life journey.

The importance of embracing change as a catalyst for personal growth.

Embracing change is essential as a catalyst for personal growth because it brings new opportunities, challenges, and experiences that can lead to transformative and positive development. Change is an inevitable part of life, and resisting it can hinder personal progress and limit one's potential. Here are some key reasons why embracing change is crucial for personal growth:

Adaptability and resilience: Embracing change helps individuals become more adaptable and resilient. When we face new situations, we are forced to stretch beyond our comfort zones, learn new skills, and develop coping mechanisms. These experiences build our ability to navigate through life's ups and downs with greater ease and grace.

Learning and self-discovery: Change often requires us to learn and acquire new knowledge. Whether it's a new job, a different environment, or a shift in personal circumstances, change forces us to explore and understand different aspects of ourselves and the world around us. Through this process of self-discovery, we gain insights into our strengths, weaknesses, passions, and areas for improvement.

Breaking limiting patterns: Embracing change can break us free from limiting patterns and beliefs that may be holding us back. It encourages us to question our assumptions, challenge our comfort zones, and step into unfamiliar territories where personal growth flourishes.

Building confidence: Successfully navigating through changes can boost self-confidence. Each time we conquer a new challenge or adapt to a novel situation, we gain confidence in our ability to handle future changes. This growing self-assurance becomes a powerful asset in pursuing our goals and dreams.

Expanding perspectives: Change often exposes us to diverse perspectives, cultures, and ideas. This exposure fosters open-mindedness and broadens our understanding of the world. An expanded perspective enables us to approach situations with empathy, creativity, and a willingness to collaborate with others.

Overcoming fear: Change can be intimidating and scary, especially when it involves leaving our comfort zones. However, by embracing change, we learn to confront and overcome our fears, which can be a significant barrier to personal growth. As we conquer these fears, we become more courageous and open to taking calculated risks.

Staying relevant and competitive: In today's fast-paced and dynamic world, change is constant, and industries evolve rapidly. Embracing change allows individuals to stay relevant, continuously develop new skills, and remain competitive in their personal and professional lives.

Fostering resilient mindset: A mindset that embraces change as an opportunity for growth encourages us to see failures and setbacks as learning experiences. It helps us bounce back more quickly from disappointments and setbacks, propelling us forward on our personal development journey.

In conclusion, embracing change as a catalyst for personal growth is crucial for leading a fulfilling and enriched life. It empowers us to evolve, learn, and become the best versions of ourselves. By remaining open to change, we can better navigate life's uncertainties and turn challenges into stepping stones toward our personal aspirations and aspirations.

Tips for developing adaptability and thriving in times of uncertainty.

Developing adaptability and thriving in times of uncertainty is a valuable skillset that can lead to personal and professional growth. Here are some tips to help you navigate uncertain situations and emerge stronger:

Cultivate a growth mindset: Embrace challenges as opportunities for learning and development. View failures as stepping stones toward improvement rather than obstacles. A growth mindset helps you stay open to new possibilities and encourages continuous improvement.

Stay flexible and open-minded: Be willing to let go of old ways of doing things and adapt to new circumstances. Avoid being rigid in your thinking or approach. Remain open to different perspectives and be ready to adjust your plans as needed.

Focus on what you can control: Uncertain times may bring many variables beyond your control. Instead of getting overwhelmed by them, concentrate on the aspects you can control. This will help you direct your efforts effectively and reduce stress.

Practice resilience: Build your resilience by developing coping mechanisms to bounce back from setbacks. Engage in activities that promote emotional well-being, such as regular exercise, mindfulness practices, or spending time with loved ones.

Break tasks into manageable steps: When faced with uncertainty, tackling large projects or challenges can feel daunting. Break them down into smaller, achievable tasks. This approach allows you to make steady progress and maintain a sense of accomplishment.

Seek knowledge and information: Stay informed about the situation you are facing. Gather reliable information from reputable sources, which will enable you to make informed decisions and plan effectively.

Build a support network: Surround yourself with supportive and like-minded individuals. Having a strong network can provide encouragement, insights, and potential solutions during uncertain times.

Embrace creativity and innovation: Uncertainty often requires thinking outside the box. Be open to trying new ideas, experimenting with different approaches, and being innovative in problem-solving.

Learn from past experiences: Reflect on how you've handled previous uncertain situations. Identify what worked well and what could have been improved. Apply these lessons to your current challenges.

Set realistic goals: In times of uncertainty, setting achievable and adaptable goals is essential. Be flexible with your timeline and be prepared to adjust your goals as circumstances change.

Take calculated risks: While uncertainty can be intimidating, it also presents opportunities for growth. Assess potential risks and rewards, and be willing to take calculated risks to move forward.

Maintain a positive outlook: A positive mindset can help you stay motivated and resilient during challenging times. Focus on the possibilities and opportunities that uncertainty brings rather than dwelling on the negatives.

Practice adaptability daily: Embrace small changes in your daily life to build your adaptability muscle. Try new activities, take different routes, or explore new interests regularly.

Accept and manage emotions: Uncertain times can trigger various emotions, such as anxiety and fear. It's essential to acknowledge these feelings and find healthy ways to manage them, such as through journaling or talking to a supportive friend or professional.

Celebrate your progress: Recognize and celebrate your achievements, even the small ones. Acknowledging your progress can boost your confidence and motivation to keep adapting and thriving.

Remember, developing adaptability takes time and practice. Be patient with yourself and allow room for growth. By implementing these tips, you'll be better equipped to navigate uncertainty and embrace the opportunities it presents.

THE CONCEPT OF A GROWTH MINDSET IN FACING NEW CHALLENGES.

The concept of a growth mindset, popularized by psychologist carol dweck, refers to the belief that one's abilities and intelligence can be developed and improved over time with effort, dedication, and learning. In contrast, a fixed mindset is the belief that one's qualities and talents are static and unchangeable, leading to the assumption that success or failure is predetermined.

When facing new challenges, individuals with a growth mindset embrace these situations as opportunities for learning and growth. They see challenges as a chance to expand their skills and knowledge, rather than as threats to their self-worth or intelligence. Here are some key aspects of a growth mindset in facing new challenges:

Embracing challenges: People with a growth mindset actively seek out challenges and view them as a natural part of the learning process. They understand that tackling new and difficult tasks is essential for personal and intellectual development.

Persistence in the face of setbacks: A growth mindset encourages individuals to persevere when encountering obstacles or failures. Instead of giving up easily, they view setbacks as opportunities to learn and improve. They see failures as temporary setbacks and believe that they can find new strategies to overcome them.

Effort and hard work: Individuals with a growth mindset recognize that effort is a crucial factor in achieving success. They understand that putting in dedicated effort and seeking continuous improvement can lead to higher levels of achievement.

Learning from criticism: Rather than feeling threatened by criticism, those with a growth mindset see it as valuable feedback that can help them grow and improve. They are open to constructive feedback and use it as a tool to enhance their skills.

Inspired by others' success: Instead of feeling envious or threatened by the success of others, people with a growth mindset see it as an inspiration. They believe that if others can achieve greatness through hard work and dedication, they can too.

Emphasis on the process: Individuals with a growth mindset focus on the process of learning and growing, rather than solely on the end result. They understand that the journey toward mastery is a continuous process that involves continuous learning and development.

Ditching the fear of failure: A growth mindset helps people overcome the fear of failure because they realize that failure is not a reflection of their inherent abilities but a stepping stone on the path to success.

By adopting a growth mindset, individuals become more resilient, adaptable, and motivated to take on new challenges. This mindset fosters a love for learning and a willingness to stretch beyond one's comfort zone, ultimately leading to personal and professional growth.

CHAPTER SEVEN

NURTURING POSITIVE RELATIONSHIPS

Nurturing positive relationships is essential for personal happiness, emotional well-being, and overall life satisfaction. Whether it's with family, friends, romantic partners, or colleagues, healthy and positive relationships contribute significantly to our social support network and provide a sense of belonging. Here are some tips on how to nurture positive relationships:

Effective communication: Open and honest communication is the foundation of any healthy relationship. Be a good listener, express your thoughts and feelings clearly, and show empathy and understanding towards the other person's perspective.

Respect and empathy: Treat others with respect, kindness, and empathy. Put yourself in their shoes and try to understand their emotions and experiences.

Quality time: Spend quality time together, whether it's through shared activities, conversations, or simply being present. Quality time helps deepen the bond between individuals.

Support and encouragement: Be supportive of each other's goals, dreams, and aspirations. Celebrate successes and offer encouragement during challenging times.

Resolve conflicts constructively: Conflicts are natural in any relationship, but it's important to handle them with respect and maturity. Focus on finding solutions and compromise rather than winning the argument.

Forgiveness and letting go: Holding grudges can damage relationships. Learn to forgive and let go of past mistakes, and encourage others to do the same.

Show appreciation: Express gratitude and appreciation for the little things the other person does. Feeling valued and appreciated strengthens the relationship.

Maintain trust: Trust is the cornerstone of a strong relationship. Be reliable, honest, and keep your promises to build and maintain trust.

Respect boundaries: Everyone has their own boundaries, and it's important to respect them. Communicate openly about your boundaries and be mindful of others' limits.

Be a positive influence: Positivity is contagious. Be someone who uplifts others and brings positivity into their lives.

Avoid assumptions: Instead of making assumptions, ask for clarification if something is unclear or bothersome. Misunderstandings can be avoided through clear communication.

Celebrate differences: Embrace the fact that people are unique with different perspectives, values, and interests. Learn from each other and celebrate these differences.

Apologize when necessary: If you make a mistake, take responsibility for it, and sincerely apologize. This shows humility and a willingness to grow in the relationship.

Share responsibilities: In any relationship, it's essential to share responsibilities and avoid burdening one person with all the tasks.

Stay connected: Even in the busiest of times, make an effort to stay connected with your loved ones. Regular communication helps strengthen relationships.

Remember that building positive relationships takes time and effort from both parties involved. By nurturing and investing in your relationships, you create a supportive and loving environment that benefits everyone involved.

THE INFLUENCE OF RELATIONSHIPS ON PERSONAL GROWTH.

Relationships play a significant role in shaping personal growth and development. They have a profound impact on individuals' emotional, psychological, and social well-being. Here are some ways in which relationships influence personal growth:

Emotional support: Healthy relationships provide emotional support during challenging times, reducing feelings of isolation and loneliness. Having someone to lean on can foster resilience and coping mechanisms, enabling individuals to navigate life's difficulties more effectively.

Self-reflection: Interactions with others often lead to self-reflection and self-awareness. Through relationships, we receive feedback and gain insights into our strengths and weaknesses, helping us understand ourselves better and identify areas for personal growth.

Learning and exposure: Relationships expose us to new ideas, perspectives, and experiences. Engaging with diverse individuals exposes us to different cultures, beliefs, and values, broadening our horizons and promoting open-mindedness.

Personal development goals: Supportive relationships can encourage us to set and pursue personal development goals. Whether it's a friend, family member, or partner, having someone who believes in our potential can be a powerful motivator.

Accountability: Healthy relationships often involve mutual accountability. When we have someone who holds us accountable for our actions and decisions, we are more likely to stay committed to our personal growth journey.

Conflict resolution: Disagreements and conflicts are inevitable in any relationship. Learning how to navigate conflicts constructively fosters emotional intelligence, communication skills, and problem-solving abilities.

Building empathy: Relationships provide an opportunity to practice empathy and understand the feelings and perspectives of others. Developing empathy enhances emotional intelligence and strengthens interpersonal connections.

Self-esteem and confidence: Positive relationships contribute to higher self-esteem and increased confidence. Feeling valued and supported by others helps individuals develop a stronger sense of self-worth.

Emotional regulation: Intimate relationships, such as romantic partnerships, can be especially influential in helping individuals learn emotional regulation and manage their emotions effectively.

Social skills: Interacting with others improves social skills, such as communication, active listening, and conflict resolution, which are essential for personal and professional success.

Encouragement of personal growth: Healthy relationships foster an environment where personal growth is encouraged and celebrated. When individuals feel safe to explore and evolve, they are more likely to embrace change and self-improvement.

It's important to note that not all relationships have a positive impact on personal growth. Toxic or unhealthy relationships can hinder personal development, leading to negative consequences. Therefore, it's crucial to cultivate and maintain healthy, supportive connections to maximize the positive influence of relationships on personal growth.

Advice on cultivating healthy and supportive relationships with family, friends, and colleagues.

Cultivating healthy and supportive relationships with family, friends, and colleagues is essential for personal growth and well-being. Here are some pieces of advice to help you foster positive connections with the people in your life:

Communication is key: Open and honest communication is the foundation of any healthy relationship. Be willing to listen actively, express your feelings and thoughts clearly, and be open to receiving feedback without defensiveness.

Show empathy and understanding: Try to put yourself in the other person's shoes and understand their perspective. Empathy fosters compassion and creates a deeper bond between individuals.

Respect boundaries: Everyone has their boundaries and comfort zones. Be mindful of respecting those boundaries and avoid pushing people into uncomfortable situations.

Be supportive and reliable: Show genuine interest in the well-being of your family, friends, and colleagues. Offer your support when needed and be reliable in keeping your commitments.

Resolve conflicts constructively: Conflicts are inevitable in any relationship. When they arise, approach them with a problem-solving mindset rather than resorting to blame or criticism. Seek to find common ground and compromise.

Celebrate successes and milestones: Acknowledge and celebrate the accomplishments and milestones of the people you care about. This shows that you value and take pride in their achievements.

Apologize and forgive: We all make mistakes, and it's important to take responsibility for them. If you hurt someone, apologize sincerely. Likewise, be willing to forgive others when they apologize.

Practice active listening: Pay attention to what others are saying without interrupting or rushing to respond. Active listening demonstrates respect and helps you understand their feelings and needs better.

Avoid gossip and negativity: Refrain from engaging in gossip or spreading negativity about others. Instead, focus on promoting a positive and uplifting atmosphere in your relationships.

Be patient and understanding: Building strong relationships takes time, effort, and patience. Don't expect instant results; allow your connections to grow organically.

Respect diverse opinions: People have different backgrounds, beliefs, and opinions. Be respectful of these differences and engage in constructive discussions rather than trying to impose your views.

Offer help and support: Be there for your family, friends, and colleagues during challenging times. Offer your help and support without expecting anything in return.

Maintain a healthy work-life balance: Ensure you have enough time for your personal life, which includes nurturing your relationships. Avoid letting work-related stress or commitments overshadow the importance of spending time with loved ones.

Practice gratitude: Express gratitude and appreciation for the people in your life. Small gestures, such as saying "Thank you" Or showing acts of kindness, can go a long way in strengthening your connections.

Be authentic: Be yourself and encourage others to be authentic as well. Authenticity builds trust and fosters deeper connections.

Remember that building and maintaining healthy relationships is an ongoing process. It requires effort, understanding, and a willingness to grow together. By investing time and energy into your relationships with family, friends, and colleagues, you can create a supportive and enriching social network that enhances your overall happiness and fulfillment.

THE SIGNIFICANCE OF SETTING BOUNDARIES AND SURROUNDING ONESELF WITH LIKE-MINDED INDIVIDUALS.

Setting boundaries and surrounding oneself with like-minded individuals hold significant importance for personal growth, well-being, and success in various aspects of life. Let's explore each aspect separately:

1. SETTING BOUNDARIES:

Boundaries are guidelines or limits we establish to protect our physical, emotional, and mental well-being. They define what is acceptable and unacceptable in our interactions with others and ourselves. Here's why setting boundaries is crucial:

Maintaining self-respect: Boundaries communicate to others that we value ourselves and expect to be treated with respect. This, in turn, helps build self-esteem and confidence.

Healthy relationships: Setting boundaries is essential for maintaining healthy relationships. It prevents us from being taken advantage of or becoming enmeshed in codependent dynamics.

Reducing stress: When we set boundaries, we reduce unnecessary stress by avoiding overwhelming commitments or toxic relationships that drain our energy.

Enhancing communication: Boundaries promote open and honest communication. They allow us to express our needs and concerns, fostering understanding and empathy.

Focusing on priorities: Setting boundaries helps us prioritize our time and energy on activities and people that align with our values and goals.

2. SURROUNDING ONESELF WITH LIKE-MINDED INDIVIDUALS:

The people we choose to spend time with can significantly influence our attitudes, beliefs, and behaviors. Being around like-minded individuals who share similar values and interests can be beneficial for several reasons:

Support and encouragement: Like-minded individuals can provide support and encouragement as they understand our aspirations and struggles better, leading to increased motivation and perseverance.

Inspiration and growth: Being around people with similar goals can inspire us to achieve more and push our boundaries, leading to personal growth and self-improvement.

Positive influences: Like-minded individuals can act as positive role models, encouraging us to adopt healthy habits and positive behaviors.

Sense of belonging: Surrounding ourselves with like-minded individuals creates a sense of belonging and acceptance, reducing feelings of isolation.

Collaboration and learning: Collaborating with like-minded people can lead to valuable learning opportunities, exchange of ideas, and increased creativity.

However, it's essential to strike a balance and remain open to diverse perspectives, even when surrounding yourself with like-minded individuals. Exposure to different ideas and opinions can broaden your horizons and help you become more well-rounded in your thinking.

In summary, setting boundaries and surrounding yourself with like-minded individuals are essential for personal well-being, growth, and success. These practices enable you to navigate life more effectively, maintain healthy relationships, and foster an environment that nurtures your values and goals. Remember to stay open to new experiences and ideas, as diversity can also lead to valuable insights and personal development.

CHAPTER EIGHT

SELF-CARE AND WELL-BEING

Self-care and well-being are essential aspects of maintaining a healthy and balanced life. They involve taking deliberate actions to promote physical, mental, and emotional health and to cope with the stresses and challenges of daily life. Practicing self-care and prioritizing well-being can lead to improved overall health, increased resilience, and a greater sense of happiness and fulfillment.

Here are some key components of self-care and well-being:

pHYSICAL HEALTH:

Regular exercise: Engaging in physical activities, such as walking, jogging, yoga, or any other form of exercise, helps to keep the body fit and improves mood.

Balanced diet: Eating a nutritious and balanced diet that includes a variety of fruits, vegetables, whole grains, and lean proteins supports overall health and energy levels.

Sufficient sleep: Getting enough restful sleep is crucial for physical and mental rejuvenation.

MENTAL AND EMOTIONAL HEALTH:

Mindfulness and meditation: Practicing mindfulness and meditation can reduce stress, increase self-awareness, and improve focus and concentration.

Emotional expression: Acknowledging and expressing emotions in a healthy way, such as through journaling or talking with a trusted friend or therapist, can help manage stress and build emotional resilience.

Setting boundaries: Learning to say no and establishing healthy boundaries in personal and professional relationships is important for mental well-being.

SOCIAL CONNECTION:

Building and maintaining positive relationships with friends, family, and social groups can provide emotional support and a sense of belonging.

Engaging in social activities and connecting with others can combat feelings of isolation and loneliness.

HOBBIES AND INTERESTS:

Making time for activities that bring joy and relaxation, such as hobbies, creative pursuits, or recreational activities, can provide a sense of fulfillment and reduce stress.

AVOIDING UNHEALTHY COPING MECHANISMS:

Minimizing the use of substances like alcohol or drugs as a way to cope with stress or emotions.

Avoiding excessive consumption of negative media and information that can impact mental well-being.

SEEKING PROFESSIONAL HELP:

If needed, reaching out to a mental health professional or counselor can provide valuable support and guidance for addressing specific concerns.

Remember that self-care is individualized, and what works for one person may not be the same for another. It's essential to listen to your own needs and preferences and develop a self-care routine that suits you best.

Practicing self-care and prioritizing well-being is not selfish; it is an act of self-preservation that enables you to show up as your best self in all aspects of life. By investing in your well-being, you can enhance your ability to handle challenges, increase your overall happiness, and build resilience to face life's ups and downs.

CONCLSION

Unlocking one's potential or personal growth is a life long process. To some, it is achieved within a short time, while it might take a longer time for many to ascertain. The most important thing to keep in mind is that, anyone thriving to develop potentially must be focus and consistent. It is also important to NOTE the following. You must......

✓ Be fully aware, which is the first step.

✓ Must have a growth mindset.

✓ Be ready to embrace changes.

✓ Set achievable and realistic goals.

✓ Cultivate resilience.

✓ Find a professional support or a mentor.

✓ Emphasize on continuous learning.

✓ Build meaningful relationships. With this, back it up with hard-work and you will have great result.

THANK YOU FOR READING AND SEE YOU AT THE TOP.

OTHER BOOKS BY TOM MANUEL

10 Smoothies For Quick Weight Lose

As Courageous As The Eagle

12 Months Period Temperature Logbook

Turning Yourself Into Cash Breathing Machine

www.ingramcontent.com/pod-product-compliance
Lightning Source LLC
Chambersburg PA
CBHW060006300526
45794CB00003B/1111